A Dorling Kindersley Book

Note to Parents

My First Look at Home is designed to help young children learn about everyday objects found in the home. It's a book for you and your child to share and enjoy – looking at the pages together, finding familiar objects, discovering where they belong, and learning and using new words.

Senior Editor Jane Yorke
Art Editor Toni Rann
Designer Jane Coney
Editorial Director Sue Unstead
Art Director Colin Walton
Photography Karl Shone
Additional photgraphy Dave King, Stephen Oliver, Stephen Shott, Kim Taylor
Series Consultant Neil Morris

Cutlery provided by David Mellor, London

First published in Great Britain in 1990
by Dorling Kindersley Publishers Limited,
9 Henrietta Street, London WC2E 8PS
Reprinted 1990

A CIP catalogue record for this book is available from the British Library.

ISBN 0-86318-461-8

Phototypeset by Flairplan Phototypesetting Ltd, Ware, Hertfordshire
Reproduced in Hong Kong by Bright Arts
Printed in Italy by L.E.G.O.

· MY · FIRST · LOOK · AT ·

Home

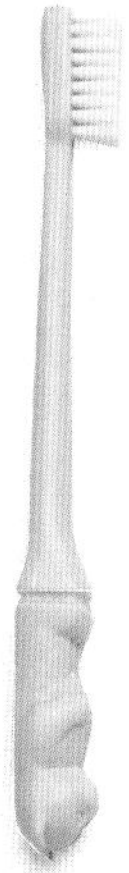

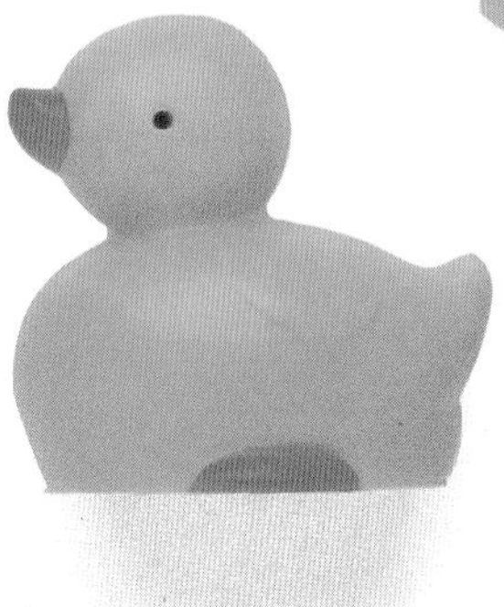

DK

DORLING KINDERSLEY • LONDON

Kitchen
We cook in the kitchen.
eggs
tomatoes
cheese grater
whisk
pasta
sharp knife
wooden spoon
rolling pin
saucepan

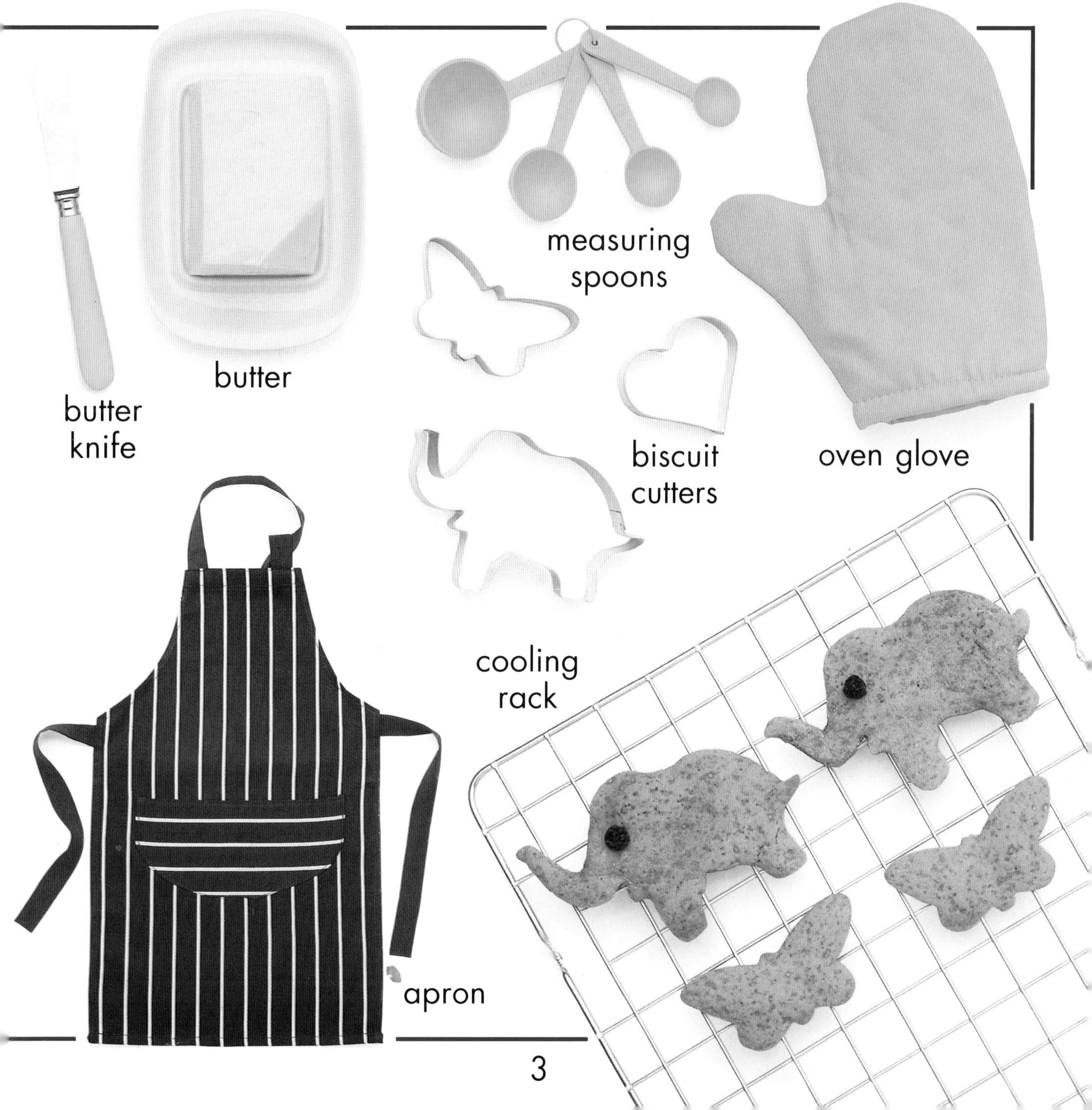
butter knife
butter
measuring spoons
biscuit cutters
oven glove
cooling rack
apron

Dining room

We eat our meals in the dining room.

mug

child's cup

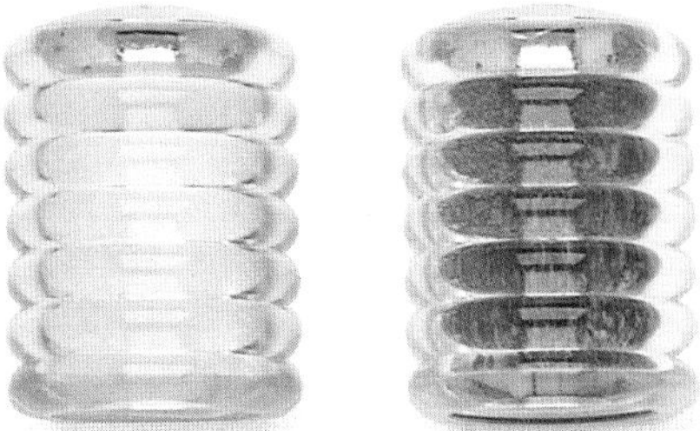

salt and pepper pots

napkin

plate

fork

knife

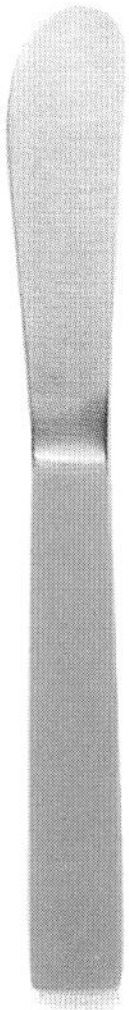

bread
basket

spoon

fruit salad

basket of
fruit

glasses

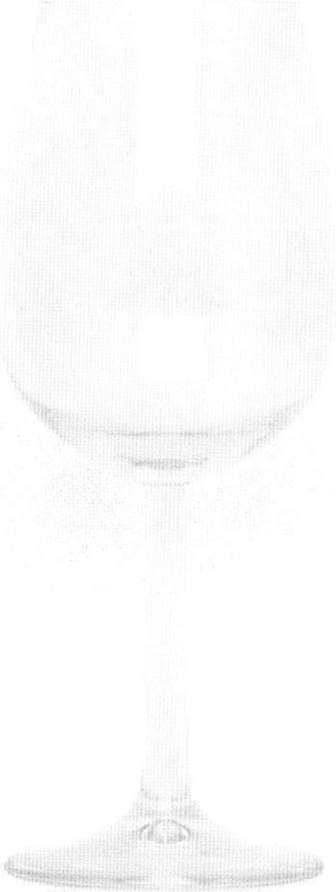

Playroom

We have fun in the playroom.

spinning top

puzzle

push-along toy

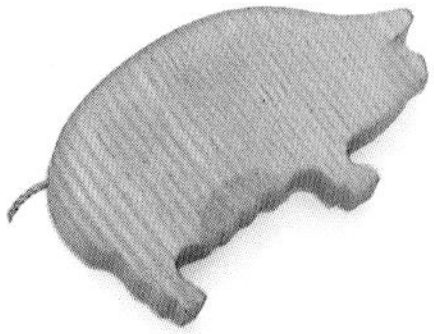

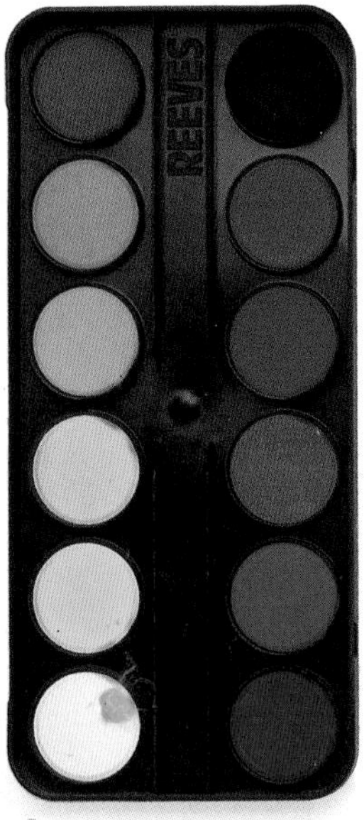

paintbox

brushes

wooden farm animals

plane
clown
bricks
drum
crayons
train

Bathroom

We wash in the bathroom.

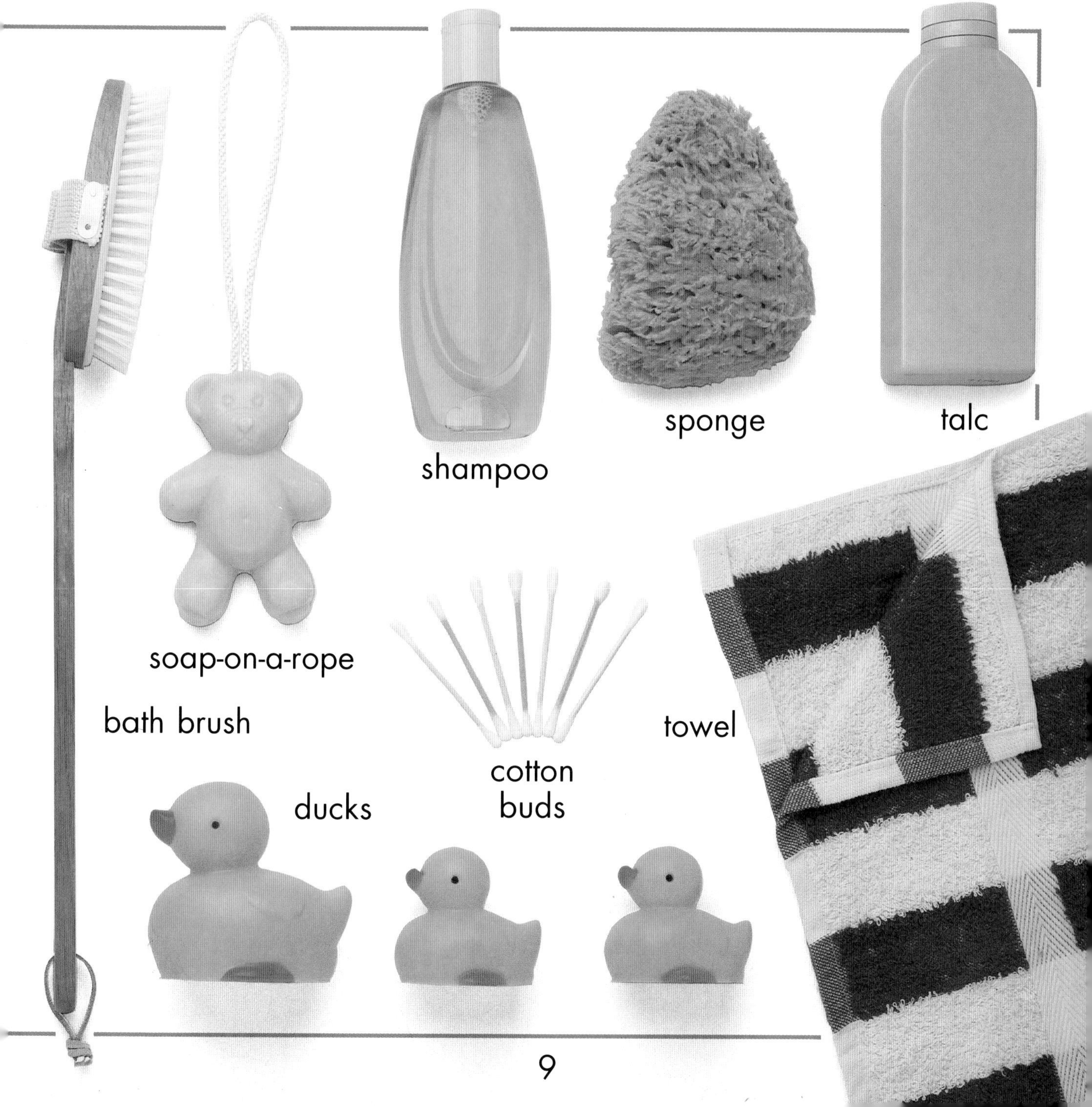
shampoo
sponge
talc
soap-on-a-rope
bath brush
towel
cotton buds
ducks

Bedroom

We sleep in the bedroom.

teddy bear

alarm clock

storybook

pyjamas

blanket

mobile

slippers

pillow

dressing gown

lamp

Garage

The car is kept in the garage.

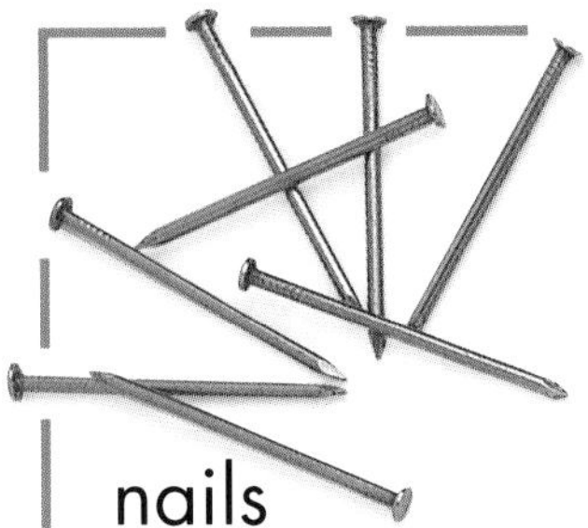

nails

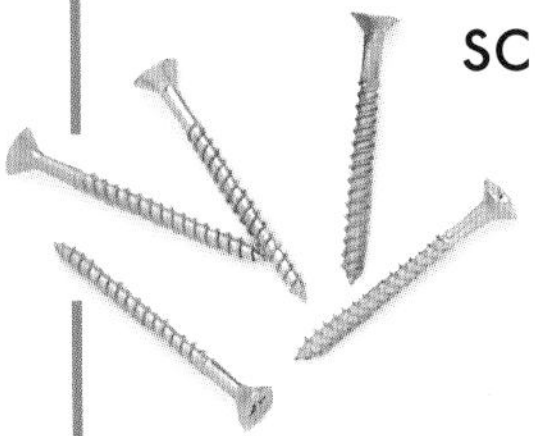

screws

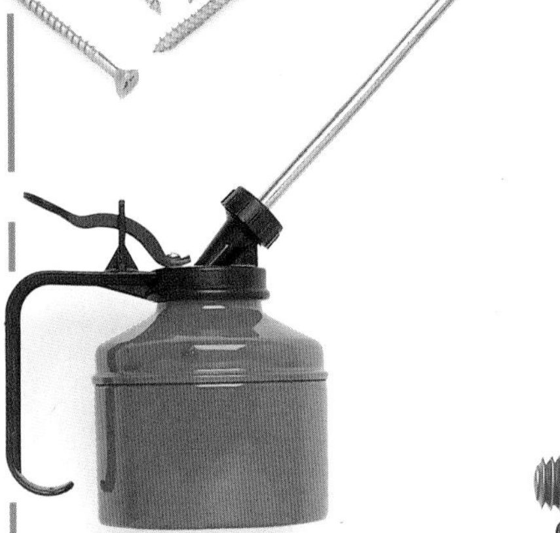

oilcan

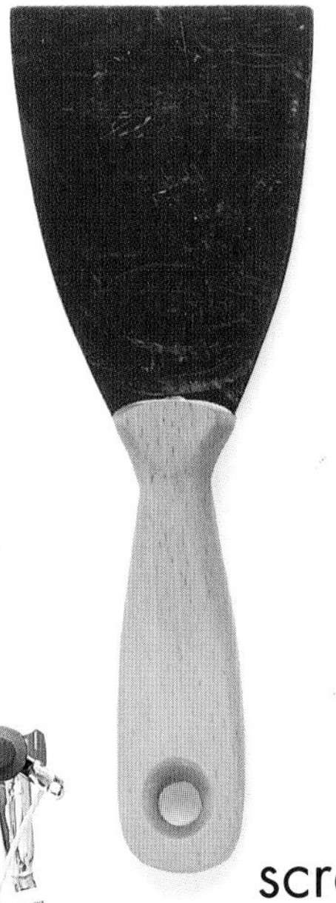

scraper

paint tin

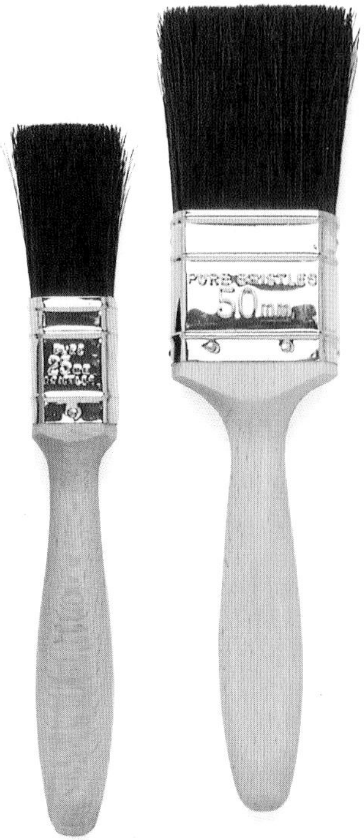

brushes

bike

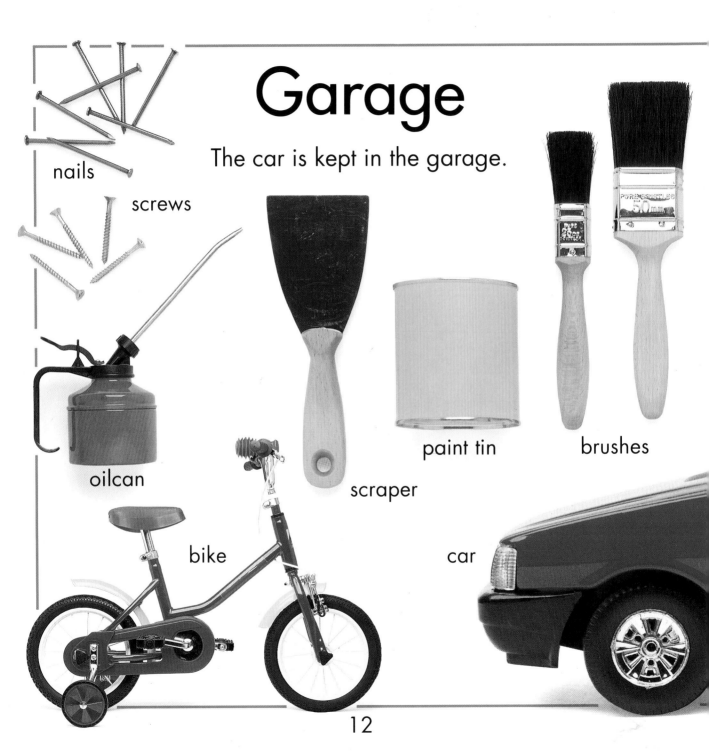

car

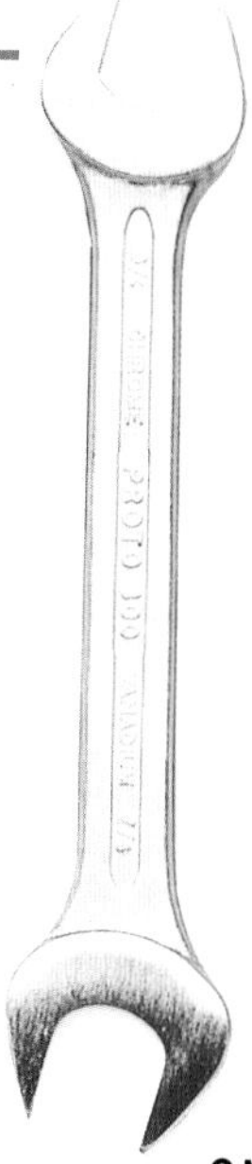

screwdriver

toolbox

spanner

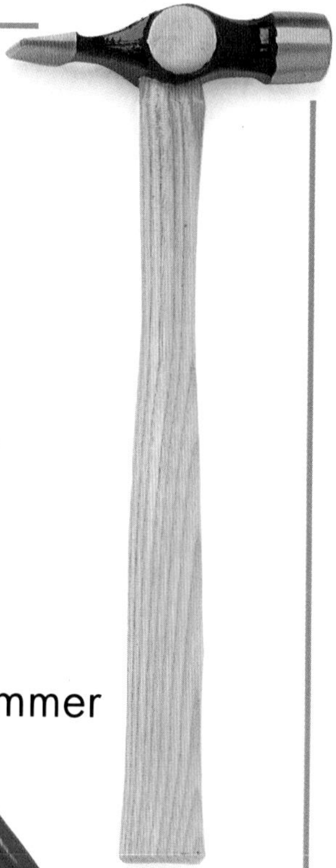

hammer

Garden

Flowers and plants grow in the garden.

spade

bucket

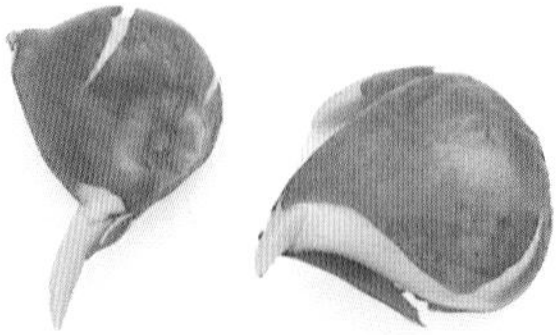

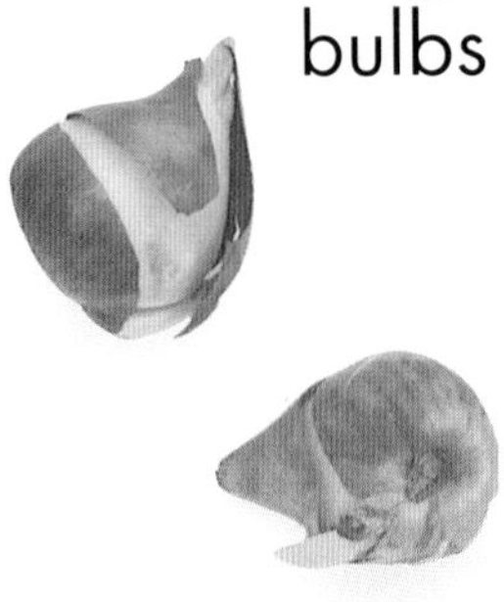

bulbs

seeds

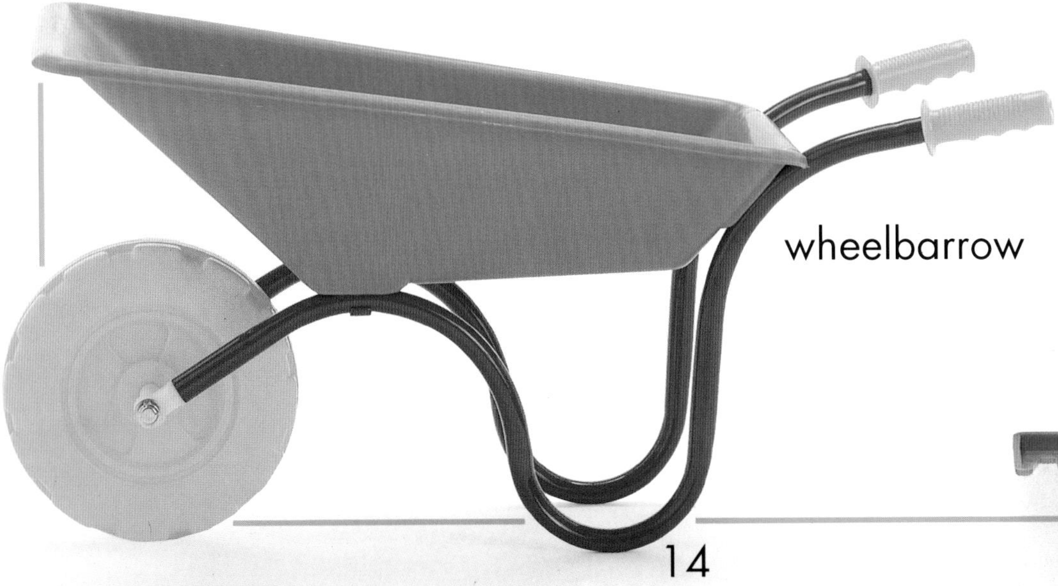

wheelbarrow

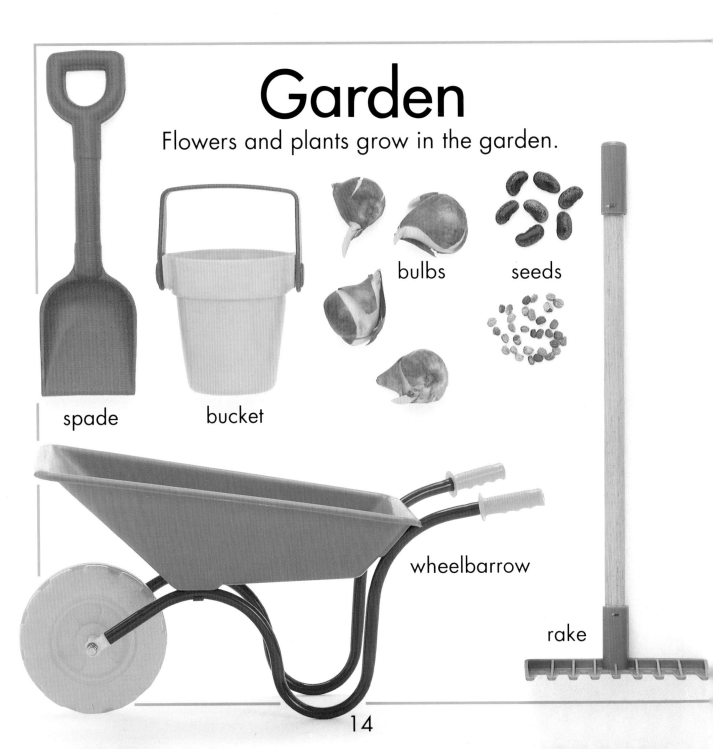

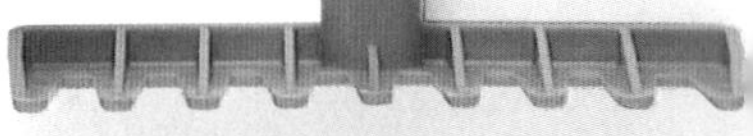

rake

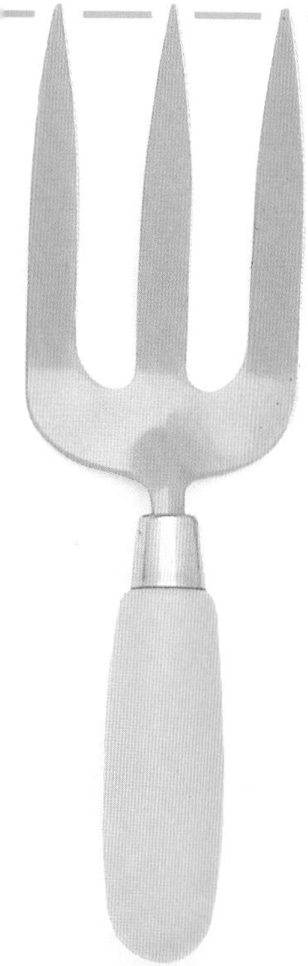

fork

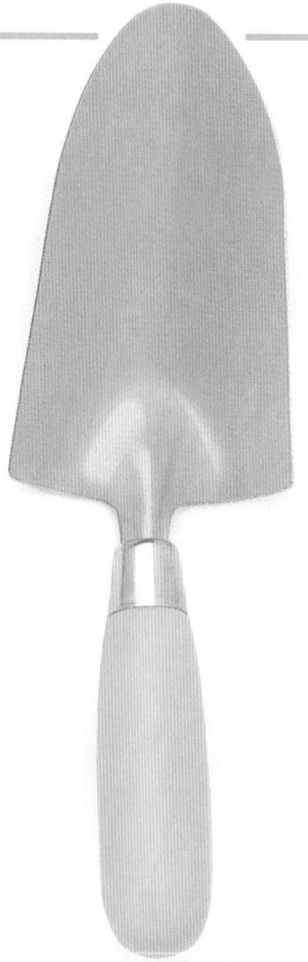

trowel

watering can

bird

plant

bird feeder

pot

snail

Can you remember?

Where do these things belong?

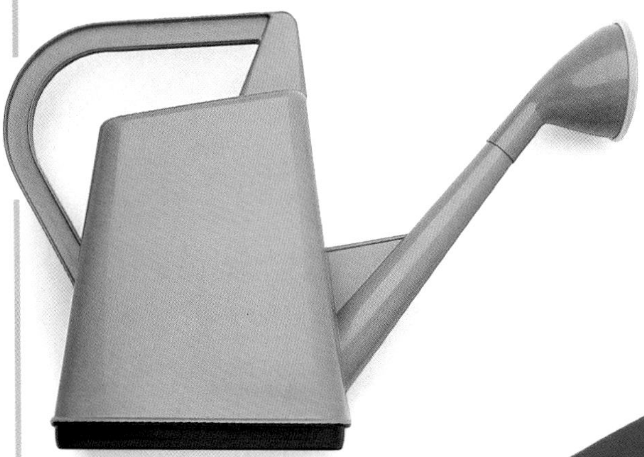

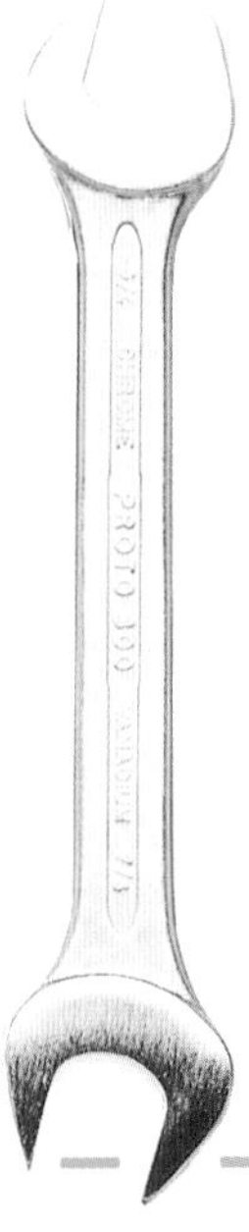